Rest and Release

A 4-WEEK BIBLE STUDY

By Courtney Joseph

Welcome to Good Morning Girls! We are so glad you are joining us.

God created us to walk with Him, to know Him, and to be loved by Him. He is our living well, and when we drink from the water He continually provides, His living water will change the entire course of our lives.

Jesus said: "Whoever drinks of the water that I will give him will never be thirsty again. The water that I will give him will become in him a spring of water welling up to eternal life." ~ John 4:14 (ESV)

So let's begin.

The method we use here at GMG is called the **SOAK** method.

- ❒ **S**—The S stands for *Scripture*—Read the chapter for the day. Then choose 1-2 verses and write them out word for word. (There is no right or wrong choice—just let the Holy Spirit guide you.)

- ❒ **O**—The O stands for *Observation*—Look at the verse or verses you wrote out. Write 1 or 2 observations. What stands out to you? What do you learn about the character of God from these verses? Is there a promise, command or teaching?

- ❒ **A**—The A stands for *Application*—Personalize the verses. What is God saying to you? How can you apply them to your life? Are there any changes you need to make or an action to take?

- ❒ **K**—The K stands for *Kneeling in Prayer*—Pause, kneel and pray. Confess any sin God has revealed to you today. Praise God for His word. Pray the passage over your own life or someone you love. Ask God to help you live out your applications.

SOAK God's word into your heart and squeeze every bit of nourishment you can out of each day's scripture reading. Soon you will find your life transformed by the renewing of your mind!

Walk with the King!

Courtney

WomenLivingWell.org, GoodMorningGirls.org

Join the GMG Community

WomenLivingWell.org | GoodMorningGirls.org

Facebook.com/WomenLivingwell | Facebook.com/GoodMorningGirlsWLW

Instagram.com/WomenLivingWell   #GoodMorningGirls

GMG Bible Coloring Chart

COLORS	KEYWORDS
PURPLE	God, Jesus, Holy Spirit, Saviour, Messiah
PINK	women of the Bible, family, marriage, parenting, friendship, relationships
RED	love, kindness, mercy, compassion, peace, grace
GREEN	faith, obedience, growth, fruit, salvation, fellowship, repentance
YELLOW	worship, prayer, praise, doctrine, angels, miracles, power of God, blessings
BLUE	wisdom, teaching, instruction, commands
ORANGE	prophecy, history, times, places, kings, genealogies, people, numbers, covenants, vows, visions, oaths, future
BROWN/GRAY	Satan, sin, death, hell, evil, idols, false teachers, hypocrisy, temptation

TABLE OF CONTENTS

INTRODUCTION

It had been a month since I had slept through the night without waking too early and letting my mind race. Due to emotional stress, I had lost about 15 pounds in 30 days and I struggled each morning to put one foot in front of the other. The shock of my husband moving out and my world turning completely upside down, did not change the fact that I had a full calendar. I had children to homeschool, meals to cook, and holidays to make special for the kids. I also had an online Bible Study to lead, as we began our study through the book of Job.

I remember hitting the red button to stop recording my Youtube for the study in Job. I smiled throughout the video and the minute I stopped the recording, I literally broke down in tears. Then I gave thanks to God that he held me throughout that video. He gave me words and strength to smile, in the midst of my very personal and private mess I was facing.

In time, days turned to months and months turned to seasons and seasons turned to a complete year passing. 2016 was the darkest year of my life and yet it was also my most intimate year with Jesus. It is out of that year of learning how to rest and release, that this study is written.

For years, I have practiced rhythms and routines in my home to maintain my walk with Jesus. It was these habits that were formed during the good times that maintained my emotional, mental, physical and spiritual life during the worst of times. So whether you are going through a happy season or hard season—this study is for you.

If your calendar is full and you feel tense, rushed and even panicked at times—this study is for you. We must stop overbooking ourselves and slow down to meditate on God's Word and let the Psalms comfort us, the Proverbs counsel us, the Gospels draw us nearer to Jesus, and Revelation fill our hearts with hope.

God wants you to talk with Him about your struggles, pains, and frustrations, and give Him all your cares in exchange for His peace.

Because we do not rest, we miss hearing God's voice. Psalm 23 comes to mind. "The Lord is my shepherd; I shall not want. He makes me lie down in green pastures. He leads me beside still waters. He restores my soul. He leads me in paths of righteousness for his name's sake."

Are you experiencing the green pastures, the quiet waters, and the restoration of your soul that Psalm 23 speaks of, from resting with your Shepherd?

Remember how the crowds pressed in on Jesus everywhere He went? Everywhere He turned, there was a need unmet, and though there was so much to do . . . He withdrew to rest.

Luke 5:16 says, "But he would withdraw to desolate places and pray."

If Jesus needed alone time with God, then certainly we do. Just think of the wisdom He wants to impart to you, the strength and the peace you may be missing out on.

Give yourself permission not to have your to-do list all checked off in order for you to rest and get alone with God.

Each weekday, I will provide for you a verse of the day, a short devotional, a reflection question and a daily scripture reading. Also, online at *WomenLivingWell.org* you will find 4 videos (one per week) that correspond with the scripture we are studying each week.

Each week I will provide for you a practical challenge of something I do in my home that helps me rest and live blessed. I hope you will take the challenges. They do make a difference!

I pray that your time spent in God's Word will lead you to rest for your soul and release of your burdens, so you can live a life of peace and freedom in Christ no matter what you are facing.

Join me on this journey, as we walk with the King.

Courtney

Week 1: Stop

One definition of the word "rest" is to stop working or movement in order to relax, refresh and recover strength.

Are you tired and weary?

Are you exhausted mentally, emotionally, or physically?

Stop.

It's time to stop working. Stop movement. Relax. Refresh. Recover. And release. It's time to rest.

But how? How can we do this in the midst of real life with really full calendars, really full to-do lists, and real people with real needs right in front of us?

15 minutes a day. Commit to giving the Lord 15 minutes a day to follow through on the scripture readings, prayers and challenges in this study. God's Word is alive and active! He will transform you as you turn to his son Jesus, the one who laid his life down for you on the cross, so you can lay your life down and find rest.

Let's get started!

WEEK 1 CHALLENGE

Go buy an extra large candle and light your candle everyday in your home. Each time the glimmer of the candle catches your eye, stop and say a prayer for peace.

I will be starting my candle in the morning but you can start yours at dinnertime or whenever is convenient for you. I will be placing mine in the kitchen—the main hub of my home.

{Share your pictures of your candle on Instagram by using the hashtags: #RestAndRelease #WomenLivingWell and #GoodMorningGirls}

DAY 1—ARE YOU DISTRACTED?

Mary sat at the Lord's feet and listened to his teaching.
Luke 10:39

Distracted. Luke 10:40 says that Martha was distracted and her distraction was called "much serving".

Does that sound like someone else you might know? Perhaps you see yourself in Martha. Martha was a good girl. She was a hard worker, she loved Jesus and she loved people. But in the process of serving, she grew anxious and troubled.

It is no mistake that the passage leading up to today's reading is of Jesus telling the parable of the Good Samaritan. Jesus emphasized the love of our neighbors but then, in the very next passage with this story of Mary and Martha, he emphasized what is even greater than loving your neighbor...loving Jesus.

In Matthew 22 Jesus says the greatest commandment is that you love the Lord your God with all your heart, mind and soul and then he says the second greatest commandment is to love your neighbor.

Have you reversed these two commandments? Have you grown distracted by serving others and missed out on following the greatest commandment, of loving God first?

Friend, what you are doing is not what is best for you. Jesus is giving you permission to stop. Rest. Sit at his feet and just listen to Him. You may not be able to change your circumstances and commitments today but determine today to begin the process of simplifying your life. Don't let another year pass of distracted living. Light your candle today and stop and pray. Jesus loves you.

Reflection Question:

What is distracting you? Is there something that is making you feel anxious or troubled? Identify it and ask the Lord for wisdom on how to release it so you can love Him more.

S—The S stands for *Scripture*

O—The O stands for *Observation*

A—The A stands for *Application*

K—The K stands for *Kneeling in Prayer*

DAY 2—WHAT SHOES ARE YOU WEARING?

For we do not wrestle against flesh and blood,
but against the spiritual forces of evil in the heavenly places.
Ephesians 6:12

A few years ago, my son began experiencing extreme foot pain when he was playing football. After every practice or game, he would come home and put his feet into ice buckets. Often, when he woke in the morning, he would not be able to walk without a noticeable limp. So we took him to the doctor and after a year of trying different techniques to alleviate the pain, he underwent surgery to insert a pin and bone graft on each foot.

Foot pain is a serious problem for a football player. Without stable footing, you are easily knocked down.

Friends, do you know why you feel like you cannot find rest? Because you are at war. Your enemy, Satan, does not want you to have peace. He wants you to run around too busy, to be with Jesus. He wants you to walk down all the wrong paths. He wants to knock you down.

Football players wear cleats so they don't slip and fall. Ephesians 6:15 tells us that part of the spiritual armor we should be wearing includes shoes fitted with the gospel of peace. The gospel is our stability. Jesus' death on the cross completely tramples over the power of Satan. We must not limp around anymore—it's time to take a stand against the enemy. What shoes are you wearing?

The shoes God has given us through the gospel offers peace, and in that peace is protection for the hard road ahead. Put on His gospel peace today and walk in it. Those shoes look great on you!

Reflection Question:

In what area do you feel like Satan keeps knocking you down? How can you take a stand against the enemy's schemes this week?

Ephesians 6:10~20

S—The S stands for ***Scripture***

O—The O stands for ***Observation***

A—The A stands for ***Application***

K—The K stands for ***Kneeling in Prayer***

DAY 3—A GREATER HARVEST

But in the seventh year there shall be a
Sabbath of solemn rest for the land.
Leviticus 25:4

Genesis tells us, God created the heavens and earth in six days and on the seventh day, He rested. God stopped.

We are made in God's image and we too need to stop. Each day we stop for about 7 hours of sleep at night. Each week we stop after six days of working to rest and worship. In the book of Leviticus, we see another hard stop—this time for the land.

In Leviticus 25, God commanded that his people work the land for six years, but in the seventh year they were to give the land a solemn rest. This rest required God's people to trust that God would provide for their needs, while the land rested.

Not only was this good for God's people to rest and trust in God, but it also was very good for the soil. Resting the soil helped to restore the nutrients that were depleted throughout the years. Nowadays, farmers rotate their crops but in Bible times, the people may not have understood how necessary it was to rest the land so that they would have a greater harvest in coming years.

Is something depleting you? Is there something you need to take a long rest from? After my difficult year in 2016, I decided that the year of 2017 would be my year of saying "no." Every ounce of the people pleaser in me felt guilty saying no to new commitments or stepping away from areas where I had consistently been dependable and a "go to girl." But I simply needed to stop.

God created his creation to require rest and dependence on him. Resting is good and can lead to a greater harvest in the future, if we will simply take God at His word.

Reflection Question:

Is there something that is depleting you that you need to take a long rest from? Pray about this concern and seek godly counsel if you are unsure.

S—The S stands for *Scripture*

O—The O stands for *Observation*

A—The A stands for *Application*

K—The K stands for *Kneeling in Prayer*

DAY 4—SHARPEN YOUR AX

*If the iron is blunt, and one does not sharpen the edge,
he must use more strength, but wisdom helps one to succeed.
Ecclesiastes 10:10*

Do you feel worn down and worn out?

Ecclesiastes uses the example of a worn out ax and how foolish it would be to keep using a dull one rather than stopping to sharpen it. You see, the more trees you try to cut down with the same ax, the longer it will take and the more strength it will require.

A dull ax leads to accidents and requires more strength than a sharp ax. A sharp ax is more efficient, productive, effortless and enjoyable to use.

Does your ax need sharpened? Have your long and extended hours of working and serving others worn you out? Do you need more skill or wisdom for life?

Wisdom tells us that when we stop and sharpen the edge of our ax, our future will be better. Sharpening the ax may take more time but it will save energy in the long run.

Perhaps you need to stop and read a book that will help you grow in an area where you are struggling—maybe in marriage, parenting, finances, home organization, or time management. Maybe you need to stop and seek wise counseling in an area where you need healing. Or maybe you just need to stop and pray and fast for a while and reconnect with your Savior. Whatever area it is that you are feeling dull, take time now to consider how you can sharpen your ax so when you hit—you hit harder.

Reflection Question:

What has worn you down? In what area of life, do you want to sharpen your ax?

S—The S stands for *Scripture*

O—The O stands for *Observation*

A—The A stands for *Application*

K—The K stands for *Kneeling in Prayer*

DAY 5—YOU NEED TIME ALONE

He went up on the mountain by himself to pray.
When evening came, he was there alone.
Matthew 14:23

During my season of rest, I also found that it was a season of withdrawal. I took a break from blogging and posting regularly on social media, and I also took a break from some of the Bible Studies I was involved in, in real life. I decided to be alone.

Withdrawing (for a social butterfly like me) has been painful at times. For those who are detoxing from something they are addicted to, the withdrawal period is painful. But we all know that those who come through the withdrawal season are always better, stronger and healthier on the other side.

I am not recommending that you drop out of your church groups, if you do not have other close Christian fellowship. During this time, I have stayed close to my family and strong Christian friends and I have a godly counselor. I am not alone. But there were some extras in there that needed to be trimmed away, just for a season, so I could experience something deeper and better for my soul. I was seeking rest and that is exactly what I received from the Lord.

After John the Baptist died, we see that Jesus withdrew to a desolate place by himself. Then again, after he fed the 5,000, Jesus withdrew alone on the mountain to pray. During emotional times of loss or a season of busyness, we need a hard stop, where we simply get alone with God to be refreshed. It may be painful to step away but the alone time with the Lord, without other voices speaking into our lives, is exactly what we need.

Reflection Question:

Are you battle weary and in need of a time of withdrawal so your soul can be restored? How can you make that happen this weekend?

S—The S stands for *Scripture*

O—The O stands for *Observation*

A—The A stands for *Application*

K—The K stands for *Kneeling in Prayer*

Video Notes

(go to WomenLivingWell.org to find the weekly corresponding videos)

Week 2: Receive God's Love

We all long to connect with others and to be seen and loved.

God is relational like us.

God wants to connect with us and be seen and loved.

God wants to be seen in all his beauty and majesty through his creation. The vast blue sky, the birds that chirp outside our windows, the meadow filled with flowers and the roaring ocean—all speak His name.

1 John 4:19 tells us, "we love because He first loved us."

God first loved you and He gave His son to die on the cross for your sins so you could have a relationship with Him. He sees you and he longs to connect with you in a deep and intimate way. Let's take time this week to bask in God's love for us. It is in knowing and receiving his love, that we are able to rest and release our burdens to him.

WEEK 2 CHALLENGE

Go pick a bouquet of flowers from your garden or a nearby field or buy yourself a small bouquet. Each time you see the flowers, be reminded of God's love for you.

I will be purchasing a small bouquet from my grocery store and placing it in a vase, in my kitchen.

{Share your pictures of your flowers on Instagram by using the hashtags: #RestAndRelease #WomenLivingWell and #GoodMorningGirls}

DAY 1—REST IN THE POTTER'S HANDS

I praise you, for I am fearfully and wonderfully made.
Psalm 139:14

Have you ever knit a sweater or blanket before? Perhaps like me—you have not, but I am sure you have made something with your hands that you loved.

Back in my twenties, I took cake-decorating classes. It was such a joy to learn how to make beautiful cakes. I remember making my grandmother a birthday cake from scratch. That cake took me hours to make. When it was finished, I put it on a glass pedestal dish and then wrapped tulle and lights around the bottom to light it up and make it extra special. It was such a joy to create!

Then in my thirties, I was really into scrapbooking. I would go on scrapbooking retreats, to scrapbooking parties and drive long distances to buy scrapbooking supplies. I had so much fun archiving our memories and those albums are my treasures.

What is something you have created? Maybe it's a painting, jewelry, a special recipe you like to cook or a garden you tend to daily. Whatever it is—because you created it—you probably love it.

Friends, you are God's creation. He made you. Isaiah 64:8 tells us that God is the potter and we are the clay. We are the work of His hands.

Psalms 139 says that he knit you together in your mother's womb. He loves you a million times more than you love the things you have created. This affection he feels for you is so much greater than our human emotion can fully grasp, but perhaps by considering some of the things you have made with your hands, for a moment you can imagine the deep affection God has for you. You can rest in the potter's hands. He deeply loves you.

Reflection Question:

What is something you have created that you love? How does understanding your affection for what you have created help you understand God's affection for you and bring you rest?

S—The S stands for *Scripture*

O—The O stands for *Observation*

A—The A stands for *Application*

K—The K stands for *Kneeling in Prayer*

DAY 2—REST IN YOUR SHEPHERD'S ARMS

*I am the good shepherd. The good shepherd
lays down his life for the sheep.
John 10:11*

Do you have a pet? Up until the age of 38, I had never had a pet—not even a fish or a frog!

But in the summer of 2014, a little white ball of fluff, rocked our world when we got our first puppy named Snowball. At first, Snowball was a lot of work as she piddled in the house, needed to be let out and in—10 times a day, barked a lot and dug in the mud. The period of adjustment was not easy for me as she added one more responsibility to my plate. But as time went on, I fell in love.

Snowball was meant to be my daughter's dog but early on she took a strong liking to me. Everywhere I went in the house she was under my feet—at my desk, on the couch, in the kitchen, under the dinner table and even on my bed.

And then there's the way she greets me when I have been away. She runs to me with her tail wagging swiftly and smothers me with kisses and love and then she does a victory lap, running around the house celebrating that I am home. Oh how I love Snowball!

Friends, John 10 tells us that God is our shepherd and we are his sheep.

We are Snowball.

We are deeply loved! Just like I love and care for Snowball, God loves and cares for you. And just like Snowball follows me around everywhere I go—we are to follow God everywhere we go and rejoice in God's presence. Let's rest in our Shepherd's good care and trust in His love for us.

Reflection Question:

How does knowing that you always have a loving guide in your life bring you rest?

S—The S stands for *Scripture*

O—The O stands for *Observation*

A—The A stands for *Application*

K—The K stands for *Kneeling in Prayer*

DAY 3—REST WITH YOUR FRIEND

Greater love has no one than this,
that someone lay down his life for his friends.
John 15:13

After my husband had moved out, I didn't know who I could trust. I wanted to tell my friends but I felt that if I had any hope of reconciling with my husband, I needed to keep our matters private. So I only told my family. But after over a month of silence, the weight loss and my disposition were giving away my secret. I had to confide in my close circle of friends because I needed them. It was scary to speak my shocking truth. No one expected it—I had always spoken highly of my husband and all of my friends knew that I adored him.

While it was scary to say out loud what was happening in my life, the tidal wave of love and support I received was exactly what I needed. Every morning I woke to a living nightmare but as I stumbled into my kitchen for coffee, there sat multiple bouquets of flowers from my friends. I felt loved.

God used those flowers to comfort me and help me feel His presence. In Matthew 6, Jesus tells us to not worry and then he uses the example of how God cares for the lilies of the field. If He takes good care of the lilies of the field then certainly He will take good care of you and me.

Jesus does not just love us as His creation and as His sheep, but Jesus loves us as a friend. He is there for us when we wake and when we are lying in bed asleep. He never leaves us nor forsakes us.

You are not alone and because He is with you—you never have to live in fear. Rest in your friendship with Jesus today. Enjoy your time with Him—He's the best friend a girl can have!

Reflection Question:

In John 15, Jesus calls you His friend. How does knowing that you always have a friend with you bring you rest?

S—The S stands for *Scripture*

O—The O stands for *Observation*

A—The A stands for *Application*

K—The K stands for *Kneeling in Prayer*

DAY 4—REST IN YOUR FATHER'S LOVING ARMS

You have received the Spirit of adoption as sons,
by whom we cry, "Abba! Father!"
Romans 8:15

The word "father" invokes powerful feelings. If you had a good father, as I have, you may feel the warmth of security and love. But if you had a distant father, an inconsistent father or a father who never hugged you, praised you or loved you—you may feel pain inside. For some, your father is not your safe place.

God is not like our earthly fathers. He is perfectly consistent, perfectly loving and perfectly kind. But Satan wants to lie to us about who God is. He does not want us to trust God or rest in His loving arms. He wants to deceive us into thinking that the Heavenly Father is just like our earthly father, so that we grow to hate God.

Today, determine to let these lies about your Heavenly Father end. Put to rest the deeply tangled web of troubles your earthly father may have caused you and turn to your heavenly Father who loves you deeper than any man will ever love you.

God wants to be your safe place. He will protect you, provide for you, guide you and gently discipline you, when you are going off the path that is best for you.

You are God's child and this is more intimate than a potter's relationship with its clay, an owner's relationship with her pet, and the relationship of two close friends. A good father has a deep affection for his child and in turn, the child has a deep affection for her father. Your God is a good good father. Rest in His loving arms today.

Reflection Question:

How does knowing that you are a child of God comfort you and bring you rest?

S—The S stands for *Scripture*

O—The O stands for *Observation*

A—The A stands for *Application*

K—The K stands for *Kneeling in Prayer*

DAY 5—REST IN YOUR GROOM'S LOVING ARMS

The two shall become one flesh. This mystery is profound,
and I am saying that it refers to Christ and the church.
Ephesians 5:31~32

The deepest and most intimate relationship on earth is that of a husband and wife. God does not just love you as his creation, as a shepherd loves his sheep, as a friend loves a friend or as a father loves his child—but he loves you as a husband loves his wife.

Oh friends, today's passage in Ephesians 5 has always been a favorite for me. God's word says that marriage is a profound mystery because it is meant to be a real life picture of Christ and the church. This is why God hates divorce—because it is a terrible picture of his everlasting covenant He has made with us. Christ laid his life down for his bride. There's no greater love than the love of our groom—Jesus!

His love is greater than any man's love. If you have a wonderful husband —rejoice and enjoy the blessing you have been given. But if you do not, do not let a man's failings destroy the intimacy God wants to have with you. God is relational. He wants to do life with you. He is pursuing you and will fight for you—even when your husband does not. Revelation 19 tells us that one day, we will see Jesus face to face at the marriage supper of the lamb. We will be His bride and he will be our groom. Oh what a glorious day that will be! But we don't have to wait to enjoy intimacy with Jesus—we can bask in that love now. Keep drawing near to Him every single day. Trust Him. He loves you so.

Reflection Question:

Is there any reason, after looking this week at how much God loves you and pursues you that you cannot rest in God? Whatever concerns you still have, take them to Jesus in prayer. Ask Him to remove the lies the enemy is telling you and give you rest.

S—The S stands for *Scripture*

O—The O stands for *Observation*

A—The A stands for *Application*

K—The K stands for *Kneeling in Prayer*

Video Notes

(go to WomenLivingWell.org to find the weekly corresponding videos)

Week 3: Release

It is only through knowing and receiving God's love, that we are able to rest and release our burdens to him. If you do not believe you are loved unconditionally, then you will feel like you have to work to please God. You'll never quite feel like you are enough and you will certainly not be able to trust him with your burdens.

We have seen from last week's study, that God loves you deeply. He's not looking for good behavior, he's looking for deeper intimacy with you. He doesn't just want to meet with you on Sunday mornings in the pew. He wants a day by day, hour by hour, minute by minute relationship with you.

Are you ready to live that way? To live like Jesus is right there with you every step of the way, always there to lighten your load?

Sometimes I feel the closest to God when I am singing worship music. There is a release that happens when we sing. Some say that singing is just as beneficial as exercise, in regards to releasing the happy endorphins in your brain. Singing lifts our spirits and relieves built up tension—so lets do what the book of Psalms tells us, and sing to the Lord. Sing out in the shower or the car or wherever you can. Let's rest and release.

WEEK 3 CHALLENGE

Determine to sing to the Lord this week.

I have a playlist I have created titled "worship music" on my iPhone. I'll be listening to it on the treadmill, in the car and in my kitchen on my blue tooth speaker and I may or may not be belting out songs to Jesus in the shower.

{Share your pictures of your worship playlist on Instagram by using the hashtags: #RestAndRelease #WomenLivingWell and #GoodMorningGirls}

DAY 1—RELEASE YOUR BURDENS THROUGH SINGING

About midnight Paul and Silas were praying and singing hymns to God suddenly there was a great earthquake, so that the foundations of the prison were shaken. And immediately all the doors were opened, and everyone's bonds were unfastened.

Acts 16:25,26

Paul and Silas were prisoners but that prison could not keep them from singing. They sang songs to the Lord and the prison doors flew open—they were free.

Friend, it is time to stop living as a prisoner to your fears, pain, sin, wounds, bitterness and bad relationships.

Release it all today. Let it go. It is time to live free.

You cannot live another day of letting yourself feel unloved. God loves you. You cannot live another day of letting yourself feel defeated. Jesus came to give us peace and set us free.

God is using whatever stress or duress in your life that you are suffering, to draw you to him today. Like a muscle that only gets stronger through lifting more weight, he wants to strengthen your faith.

So today—we not only release all of our burdens to Jesus, but we can rejoice that we have a God who loves us and takes good care of us.

Sing out to Jesus. Turn on your worship playlist and release all of that stress inside of you. The book of Psalms tells us over and over and over to sing to the Lord. Don't miss how God wants to work in your life, through your obedience to sing. When we magnify God rather than magnifying our problems, we experience God's power and peace. Pursue peace. Pursue freedom. Sing!

Reflection Question:

What is your favorite song to sing to Jesus? Why is it your favorite?

Acts 16:16~34

S—The S stands for *Scripture*

O—The O stands for *Observation*

A—The A stands for *Application*

K—The K stands for *Kneeling in Prayer*

DAY 2—RELEASE YOUR BURDENS THROUGH PRAYER

Do not be anxious about anything, but in everything by prayer and supplication with thanksgiving let your requests be made known to God.
Philippians 4:6

Every morning when our feet hit the floor, we enter into a spiritual battle. This battle began in the Garden of Eden and like it or not, it still rages on and we are a part of this epic battle. Just like we clothe ourselves everyday for whatever the day holds, we are commanded to put on our spiritual armor. This is not a suggestion. This is a command. Why? Because God knows that without our armor—we will be defeated.

Darkness is an active force. It presses and pushes its way into our lives. The light must not be passive. We cannot sit by and just let the darkness overtake us. We must fight. We must shine.

Singing is our battle cry, and God's Word is our sword. God's Word is alive, and active and God says in his Word—--to pray. God says to not be anxious about anything. Anything means...anything. But instead of being anxious, we are to pray about everything; and when we pray, God exchanges our fears and worries for peace.

Prayer is a necessity.

Without prayer, we end up surrendering to the enemy. But we want to do the opposite. We want to surrender to God and let him fight for us. This doesn't mean that our circumstances will change (although sometimes that does happen) but rather it means in the midst of our battle, we are able to stand strong.

Do not worry. Pray about everything. Nothing is too small to pray about. Release your burdens to the Lord today in prayer. Stand in victory.

Reflection Question:

What do you need to release in prayer today? Write your prayer below.

S—The S stands for *Scripture*

O—The O stands for *Observation*

A—The A stands for *Application*

K—The K stands for *Kneeling in Prayer*

DAY 3—RELEASE YOUR BURDENS THROUGH THANKSGIVING

Give thanks in all circumstances;
for this is the will of God in Christ Jesus for you.
1 Thessalonians 5:18

What we focus on grows. If we focus on our troubles—they will grow.

Recently I had something really eating at me. I thought and thought about it and the more I thought about it—the bigger it grew in my head. I sat down and pounded out an email in response to the problem. Then I slept on it. The next morning, I reread the email I had written and realized the problem had mushroomed in my mind. I needed to let it go. So I deleted the email and my life is better for it.

Have you done this before? Please say I'm not alone!

The minute I was busy doing other things and started thinking a different set of thoughts— the problem shrank and I decided to just give it to God in prayer and release it.

In 1 Thessalonians 5, we are told to rejoice always, pray without ceasing and then, in all circumstances—give thanks. After we are done singing and praying, it is God's will that we live with a thankful heart in ALL circumstances.

Dear friends, no woman dreams of growing up and becoming a single mom. My circumstances are disappointing but when I give thanks to God for the many ways he has blessed me in my life, a grateful heart grows inside of me.

Singing, praying and giving thanks—belong together. It is God's will that we live our lives this way because God knows it is best for us. Do not let your troubles grow and mushroom in your mind, instead let your singing, praying and gratefulness grow and watch how your burdens lift.

Reflection Question:

Look around the room and take time to reflect. Make a long list of things you are thankful for today.

1 Thessalonians 5:16~18

S—The S stands for *Scripture*

O—The O stands for *Observation*

A—The A stands for *Application*

K—The K stands for *Kneeling in Prayer*

DAY 4—LETTING GO OF YOUR BAGGAGE

Casting all your anxieties on him, because he cares for you.
1 Peter 5:7

I am a woman in transition right now. I have baggage. I don't mean just a little back pack—I mean I have multiple suitcases full of emotional stuff. Have you ever had a suitcase that you were trying to zip closed but the stuff kept popping out? That's me.

As a result of this, sometimes I feel like hiding because I don't even trust myself and what I might say. I don't want anyone to see my baggage. Or worse, I hate it when I'm with someone I trust and so I open my baggage a little and it starts spilling out more than I meant to. I can't zip it back closed and I walk away embarrassed because I overexposed myself.

Maybe you can relate?

We all have hurts from our childhood, maybe things done to us, or choices we made that we regret, insecurities, broken relationships, problems with our kids, financial struggles, health problems or spiritual hang ups.

We all have baggage. Don't let that fancy purse, on the shoulder of the girl who seems to have it all together, fool you. She's got junk in her purse too, just like the rest of us.

God tells us to cast our anxieties on him. The word "cast" means to literally throw something forcefully. Friends, it's time to unzip your bags and take all that you've been hiding and throw it onto the lap of God. Release it to him today. He cares for you.

Reflection Question:

What is inside your bag that you have been hiding from those around you? Take it out now and give it to God.

1 Peter 5:6~11

S—The S stands for *Scripture*

O—The O stands for *Observation*

A—The A stands for *Application*

K—The K stands for *Kneeling in Prayer*

DAY 5—LET OTHERS HELP YOU CARRY YOUR BURDENS

What you are doing is not good. You and the people with you will certainly wear yourselves out, for the thing is too heavy for you. You are not able to do it alone.
Exodus 18:17,18

It is pride that keeps us from admitting that we need God's help. Another thing that pride will do, is keep us from admitting to others that we need help.

I have always struggled to voice my needs. Feeling needy is humbling. In my pride, I want to be strong and capable. Many times I seek out answers to my problems by reading good books or blog posts but those authors don't know me personally and they can't help me carry my burdens in real life.

This year, I humbled myself and I turned to my family and friends for support. I also went to see a counselor and oh, what a blessing she has been to me. Her listening ear, her understanding of God's Word, her wisdom to navigate the messy parts of my life and her prayers at the end of our session, have been a balm for my soul.

You must stop carrying your very heavy burdens alone. God wants to lift it off of your back and many times he uses people to do that heavy lifting.

In Exodus 18, Moses tried to do his job alone and Jethro told him, that was not a good thing. It was too heavy of a load for just one man to bear and he would wear himself out. Moses listened to the counsel of Jethro and got help. Friend, do the same today. Humble yourself and get help if you need it.

Reflection Question:

Is there something in your life that you need help with? What is keeping you from getting the help you need from friends or family? If it is pride, humble yourself. If it is because you don't feel like you have anyone to turn to, pray God brings a God fearing woman into your life and until then, go see a pastor or counselor.

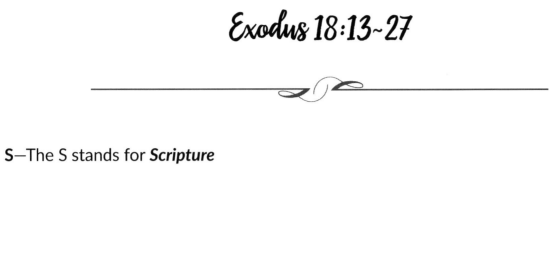

Exodus 18:13~27

S—The S stands for *Scripture*

O—The O stands for *Observation*

A—The A stands for *Application*

K—The K stands for *Kneeling in Prayer*

Video Notes

(go to WomenLivingWell.org to find the weekly corresponding videos)

Week 4: Rest

Most of us rarely surrender to our weariness. I know this because you are probably like me. I mistakenly believe I can go and go and go without consequence.

My children have very busy sports and social lives. They have high goals in many areas of their lives and keeping track of all their needs, plus running a blog, connecting with loved ones, and running my home all alone, makes for an exhausting life.

It is a blessing to live in a day and age when we have so many options and opportunities but having the courage to say no to good things is necessary.

We must learn to say no to things that will cause us to miss out on the rest we were created to need.

Need. Did you catch that?

Rest is a need—not a want. Rest is not optional or something we will do when we are 65 and retired. Rest is a blessing from the Lord that He created us to need. Needing rest—is humbling. We have to admit that we are not superhuman and that we need to depend on God for strength. We all need rest. So let's get started!

WEEK 4 CHALLENGE

Determine to sleep extra long one night this week or to take a nap or a bubble bath. This is not pampering. This is meeting your God given need for rest.

Since I have overachiever tendencies, I am going to try to do all three this week. ☺

{Share pictures of your favorite place to rest on Instagram by using the hashtags: #RestAndRelease #WomenLivingWell and #GoodMorningGirls}

DAY 1—THE SECRET TO FINDING REST

Come to me, all who are weary and burdened,
and I will give you rest."
Matthew 11:28

I read somewhere that the Chinese pictograph for busy is two characters—a heart and killing. Isn't that appropriate?

The clock ticks fast everyday as I move from breakfast dishes, to lunch dishes, to dinner dishes and then back to breakfast time once again. The calendar pages flip fast and before I know it we are saying "Happy New Year" once again!

And there at the end of the year, as I'm exhausted from holiday expectations...I feel it... the heart killing.

And so hope is restored on January 1st. When the slate feels clean and a new year begins. The idea of a second chance to slow down, rework my priorities and live well begins...but inevitably, by March, I'm defeated.

I have done it again. I have made myself too busy again. I am just so tired...again. And then Jesus. He speaks into my busy days and says, "Come to me, all who are weary and burdened, and I will give you rest."

He bids me to come...he promises rest.

He bids you to come...he promises you rest.

We have to believe that the heart killing is a real problem. Let's live with hearts that are full and alive.

Reflection Question:

What is killing your heart? What is getting in the way of you experiencing the rest that Jesus offers you today?

S—The S stands for *Scripture*

O—The O stands for *Observation*

A—The A stands for *Application*

K—The K stands for *Kneeling in Prayer*

DAY 2—BE STILL

Be still, and know that I am God.
Psalm 46:10

Be Still.

Those are two small words that pack a big punch. Being still is difficult when your world has been turned upside down by a broken relationship, a sudden illness, the loss of a loved one or any other sudden turn of events.

The stillness God wants from us is to come from a deep trust in Him. We are to be still... and know. What are we to know? That God is with us and He is in control.

Over the last year, I have faced many restless nights. I have had to remind myself over and over to be still—so I could rest. I found it physically impossible to sleep when I was crying, worrying, thinking fearful thoughts or trying to solve my own problems in my head. I had to cut it out. I had to practice self-control with my thought life.

There were three passages of scripture that I printed out and kept beside my bed to help me control my thoughts—Psalm 23, Psalm 46 and Isaiah 43:1-3. If you are having trouble sleeping at night, I recommend that you meditate on scripture. It will replace your troubled thoughts with the comforting words of God and in time you will have them memorized.

Once scripture is memorized, it's in your heart forever. God will use that scripture in your life for decades to come. He will also use that scripture in the life of others, if you will share it with them. Others will be drawn to your stillness and want to know how it is you are able to not give way to fear, in the midst of your trials. God's people should be the most restful, peaceful people on earth! We have God almighty with us carrying our burdens and giving us strength in the midst of our difficulties.

Cling to God and...Be Still.

Reflection Question:

What verse brings you peace and rest when you are worried? Do you think others can see the peace of God in you?

Psalm 46:1~11

S—The S stands for *Scripture*

O—The O stands for *Observation*

A—The A stands for *Application*

K—The K stands for *Kneeling in Prayer*

DAY 3—LET GOD RESTORE YOU

He restores my soul.
Psalm 23:3

Resting is good. Releasing is good. Music and candles and flowers are good. Sleeping is good and bubble baths are good. But if that is all we do and we miss connecting with God each day...that is not good.

We may rest our body but it is God who restores our soul. Did you used to have a fire and passion for God and then because of troubles and trials it fizzled? God wants to restore that fire in you.

In Psalm 23, we are reminded that the Lord is our shepherd. He is personal—He is YOURS! We can lie down in green pastures because he keeps us safe and secure. He leads us beside still waters so we don't fall in. He restores and refreshes our souls.

Even though we walk through dark valleys, we do not have to fear—the shadows won't hurt us. God is with us and guides us. He provides victory through our difficulties now and in the future.

Sometimes I don't like God's plans for me. Sometimes I wonder why he doesn't just fix everything because I know that He can. He is strong, mighty and powerful. He can hold the entire ocean in the palm of His hand (Isaiah 40:12) so why doesn't He just do what I ask?

Perhaps it's the other way around and He wants me...to do what He asks.

Isaiah 55:9 says that God's thoughts are so much higher than ours. I cannot possibly understand all that God is doing in my life. But this I know—my story is not over yet and neither is yours. Our shepherd is walking beside us every step of the way. We are never alone. So we can light our candles, rest, release, sing, enjoy bouquets of flowers, and bubble baths! Our shepherd's got this. Let Him restore your soul!

Reflection Question:

How has God restored your soul through your past 4 weeks in His word? Has anything changed inside of you?

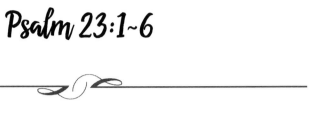

S—The S stands for *Scripture*

O—The O stands for *Observation*

A—The A stands for *Application*

K—The K stands for *Kneeling in Prayer*

DAY 4—REMEMBER WHAT GOD HAS ALREADY DONE

When you pass through the waters, I will be with you;
and through the rivers, they shall not overwhelm you;
when you walk through fire you shall not be burned,
and the flame shall not consume you.
Isaiah 43:2

One thing I am sure of, resting and releasing is not a one-time event. For the rest of our lives, we will need to work on this. Today, you may feel the weight of your burdens have been lifted but tomorrow a new trial may come and then what?

Remember.

Remember what God has already done for you and what he has brought you through in your lifetime. You are still standing and stronger than ever. Let that give you hope and peace in the future.

In Isaiah 43, we are reminded that we will go through deep waters and we will walk through the fire but we have a promise. In the midst of the waters, God will be with us. In the midst of the fire, we will not be burned.

Right now my daughter's screen saver on her phone is 2 Corinthians 4:8 which says, "We are afflicted in every way, but not crushed; perplexed, but not driven to despair."

Friends, God is with us. We may go through deep waters, we may go through the fire, we may feel afflicted and perplexed but because God has brought us through before—He will do it again! He promises He will! Do not give way to the feelings of fear or despair. Keep walking. Keep going.

Rest in God's promises and remember what God has already done for you.

Reflection Question:

What is one trial God has faithfully brought you through and how does remembering God's faithfulness remind you that you can trust him with today's trials?

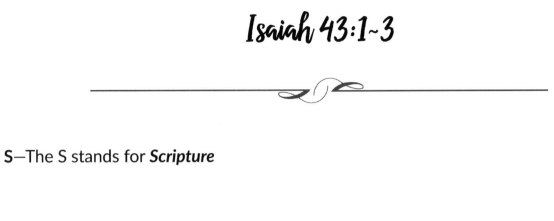

Isaiah 43:1~3

S—The S stands for *Scripture*

O—The O stands for *Observation*

A—The A stands for *Application*

K—The K stands for *Kneeling in Prayer*

DAY 5—LAUGHTER

Strength and dignity are her clothing, and she laughs at the time to come.
Proverbs 31:25

Laughter lightens the heart. It decreases stress and can alleviate pain. It is so good for the soul.

In Proverbs 31:25, we see the Proverbs 31 woman getting dressed for the day. In verse 22, we are told that she wears fine linen and purple but in verse 25 it tells us that she puts on much more than just her physical clothing. It says that she also puts on strength and dignity.

Are you dressed right now? I don't mean in just your physical clothes but have you put on strength and dignity today? Your inner rest and releasing should show on the outside. It will clothe you with strength and dignity.

Proverbs 31:25 is hanging on a plaque in my bedroom and written out on the chalkboard in my office. It inspires me to keep standing strong, keep smiling and keep laughing.

2016 was the scariest year of my life. I did not know what was going to happen to me or the kids, and I still don't know how our story will end but this I do know, laughter and fear cannot co-exist.

Some of my writing friends asked if they could come be with me the week of my court date. They wanted to be there to grieve with me. But I turned them down. Instead, I asked if they would come a few weeks later. What I really needed from my friends was to feel normal again and to laugh again.

As you continue on the path of resting and releasing your burdens to the Lord, may you live with strength and dignity. May you laugh without fear of the future. May you always trust in God every hour, every day, every season and every year, until you see your Heavenly Father face to face. He loves you so.

Keep walking with the King.

Reflection Question:

In what ways can others see your strength, dignity and inner rest? What areas do you need to work on so others can see more of God in you?

Proverbs 31:25

S—The S stands for *Scripture*

O—The O stands for *Observation*

A—The A stands for *Application*

K—The K stands for *Kneeling in Prayer*

Video Notes

(go to WomenLivingWell.org to find the weekly corresponding videos)

Made in the USA
Lexington, KY
19 September 2017